Dolor Midnight

i

DOLOR MIDNIGHT

Luciano
Iacobelli

to write away this gambling habit
too is part of the habit
obsession to know obsession
striving for perspective   positions
mind contorts   repositions itself

but pen drops

and I give up fishing barehanded in the cold str
put up the hammock and sleep outdoors

The publication of *Dolor Midnight* has been generously supported by the Canada Council for the Arts and the Ontario Arts Council.

 Canada Council   Conseil des Arts    ONTARIO ARTS COUNCIL
for the Arts   du Canada   CONSEIL DES ARTS DE L'ONTARIO

Design: Deborah Barnett
Interior images: Luciano Iacobelli

Library and Archives Canada Cataloguing in Publication

Iacobelli, Luciano, 1956-, author
     Dolor midnight / Luciano Iacobelli.

Poems.
ISBN 978-1-988254-62-3 (softcover)

     I. Title.

PS8617.A36D65 2018   C811'.6   C2018-905384-4

Published by Quattro Books Inc.
Toronto
www.quattrobooks.ca

Printed in Canada

*To those who've left
and to those who remain at the table:
Arthur, Barry, Daniel, Ewald, Gabe,
Gonzalo, John, Martin, Saro, Sam, Sasha*

Table of Contents

Prayer to the Dice

Impossible to resist you
not even a king can pass
without tripping and falling
on your stones and thorns

I was loved until I loved you
I cheated my father and my boss
stole money from my brothers
I lost my name and my friends turned
abused my daughters enjoyed my wife

I can resist you during the day
but at night resolve crumbles
in the dark I hear your rattle
and my will burns to ashes
lovesick with hope I seek you out

I am a man no one takes seriously
I dwell bankrupt under shame's feet
my only joy is the disaster of others
how everyone is pulled by failure
arrives at their own dice snatches them up
like a greedy child stealing the biggest treat

oh little cubed divinities you have
drained me of livelihood and ambition
release me now and ensnare another
pour out their self worth even the most
disciplined are steered toward fixation
empty out the next fool in line

(free translation from the Rigveda)

NOTEBOOK ONE

HOW many birds will land on the branch
which one will fly off first
toss dice in the air
and attempt to roll the weather

eclipsed man attempts
certainty by uncertain means
tests new betting schemes

sick and weak he can barely breathe or stand
the bones barely reach
the back of the table

what if the luck suddenly changes
the long awaited winning streak arrives
a lifetime of losses recovered

the thirst would stay unquenched
wagers would resume
                        debts remain unpaid
            health unrepaired

more money to wave before the snake eyes
the long-limbed disappearance
lounging in the stare

The coloured stones made the decisions
when to hunt   when to extinguish the fire
when to cross the frozen water
when to surprise the enemy

the first mind was chance implements
 pebbles
                              teeth
           acorns
astragals
tossed on the cave floor
shaken by the trembling earth

The earliest dice were simple
painted beads nuts stones
one side   black
one side   white
even odd
yes no
either or
      all or nothing

then came the more complicated cube
harder to keep honest
ivory wood metal stone plastic
        maybe loaded cogged or gaffed
                  weighted
          shaved or iced

chance has become so many sided
it is by chance that I'll discover where chance starts
where it ends

or should I set traps for the rare bird
capture it with ropes and ladders
   become many trees and move toward it
       trunk by trunk
branch by branch

beauty must be tortured first
before it confesses to a golden ratio
luck too must be broken open
      before it reveals its inner workings
why dice must be thrown over and over again
hard against a solid wall

Gambling tools are improvised quite readily
the creative mind
slopes towards
        accoutrements of chance
                        arrowheads pebbles
                        shells   sticks

slide down a snake
    climb
a ladder

short brutish nasty lives
the ancients were escape crazy
most Greek or Roman surfaces
were etched or scribbled
with layouts of board games
                    laboratories of chance

costly experiments
many sold themselves as slaves
to numb the brain
to pay their debts

Averages are fulfilled in the long term
after thousands
of flips   tosses   spins

the short term is energy disorder
            strange turns on short paths
                                    replication blunders
seven back to back midnights
double zero five times straight
ten blackjacks in succession

do not assume
that if an event happens repeatedly
a different one is imminent
the short term forgets averages
                    favours random   displacement
wild atoms an
        d molec
                ules
like love itself
exciting twists and turns of the heart
unpredictable consistencies
                betrayals

in the long term chance and passion vanish
substance concentration becomes uniform
spreads left to right diffuses through space
dilutes itself equally through empty places
drifts evenly throughout the house

until the player's pile of chips is flattened

Some say luck can be trained
you can whistle and it comes

some people attract luck
magnetic force of a person's style
the tall rather than the small
the strong jaw rather than the weak chin
the blue eye rather than the brown

floating ghost
you step into it or it steps into you
can be rubbed off
can be summoned by uttering the right word
       can be met by sitting or standing

is a horse's name
or an hour of the day a time of year
a clothes item a hat a ring
a remarkable or unremarkable occurrence

an attitudinal shift
it comes it goes
don't sit where a loser sat
   luck is sudden lightness
bad luck is a downward pull
a weight transferred from one body
to another

     you are on a great roll and some born loser
     stands next to you
and within two tosses of the dice
the bad luck lugs itself from
out his grey flesh
  and settles on your shoulders

     crap out line in
forever pay the don'ts

We carried knives nails sharp stones
scratched and scrawled swear words swastikas genitals
on school bricks garage doors we crawled
under wooden verandahs where cats gave birth
looked at pages torn from girly magazines

in the lane behind my home we watched the crap games
Spider rolled the bones he kissed them first
curly haired wiry he could burn the ground
by spitting at it could burn you by staring at you
he had hundreds in his hand

he and a circle of men throwing bills on the ground
looking out for the cops and every day there was a game
right in the middle of my play
smack in the centre of my hide and seek

a dirty nakedness to the outdoor gambling
more dangerous than the poison mushrooms
growing under the fences of nearby yards
exposed sinners these men squatting close to their bets

a gang of us pooled our dimes and nickels
sent an older kid to join the game
it only took one roll for him to lose
our childhood savings

seven come eleven
winner winner chicken dinner
box cars and pair of stars
nina nine yo and little joe
midnight and snake eyes
the poetry crawled across our young souls
sliming the polished stone

Sir is this your first time   pick up the dice with one hand
keep them over the table try to hit the back wall
avoid the stack   and don't hit the mirror
place your bets   place them now
the dice are in the air   no more bets   the point is five
fever five   mark the point   and just call out your bets
                                            press up the hard ways
                102 on the outside
horn high twelve for a quarter   dollar midnight   dollar midnight
press the five
        20 on the doctor   10 dollar yo
            dollar midnight

all bets down   dice out   no more bets   no more bets
        snake eyes
                    please sir
    don't hit the stacks

flew down for a friend's stag and the game gripped me
lost myself in the action best odds in the whole casino
they said press the hard ways a father sticks his head
in a pup tent and inhales deadly fumes the dice are in the air
the game killed my marriage but admittedly the house
had a bug problem we'd be sleeping in our bed
and cockroaches would crawl across our skin all over
our faces *dollar midnight dollar midnight*

nine nina nine hocked her last things even the ceramic
Marx Brothers figurines mom gave her for Christmas
she shed dollars pounds was lean enough to hide in one of
the game's many closets and the routine was she'd play all night
then drive back home by 7:30 shower breakfast then off to her job
at the nursing home *take me down from all the outside numbers*
soul in debt leapt from the observation deck *take the line pay in behind*

dice out   one sick puppy hangs himself with a dog leash
dice out   man wades into river
dice out   doctor jumps into the falls
dice out   man shoots himself under the boardwalk
dice out   some poor loser at the casino entrance waved a toy
            gun at the security guards worked it so he got shot

Down deep in the gambling addiction
entangled in the roots and tunnels
among the insect communities
                 a thick pink tongue
                        flapping in the soil
            mouthing debt

Atlantic City
Saturday night red eye for just 75 dollars
flight back the next morning

but if the flight was booked
there was no other way to kill the fever
but take a 16 hour bus ride to New Jersey (stopover in New York)
play 3 or 4 hours just to quell the fever
then return home be back in Toronto by Monday morning
in time to teach my first class

one summer while visiting Philadelphia
I took a side trip to Atlantic City
lost my travel money in less than an hour
had to beg for my accommodations
offered to work
                 swept the hostel clean
painted the verandah
       cleaned out the basement
for 7 days
while I waited for
my girlfriend to arrive

when she did arrive I promised her I would
never gamble again
borrowed her vacation money
and lost it too

First time in L.A.
penniless on a street bench
I lost all my vacation pay in a street corner crap game
and he sat next to me clear and liquid
I could see all the way down to the floor of his face
      the many childlike empathies and fascinations
          swimming there

what's wrong he said
I told him my story and he pitied me
said he'd replace my losses if I accompanied him to Mexico
      a black man alone he'd feel uncomfortable in Tijuana
he needed someone white to be with him
to blow his army pay with
a memorable night across the border
before home to Detroit
and bible school

I wasn't gay I told him
and he convinced me neither was he
stuffed cash in my shirt pocket
and we headed across the frontier to a ghost town
that fleshed itself only on the weekends
for the drunkards

he paid for my room and bought the girl across the hall
but not for himself it was against his religion
she was for me and besides
she probably wouldn't do it with a black man anyway
what a strange Christian he was
it broke his heart every time
a man came to her door

I declined the sickly whore
and we spent that night in various bars
and while I got drunk
he kept asking me if I was happy
              I was
and though he never touched a drink
he found a way to spin himself
into my ecstasy

next day in San Diego true to his word
he replaced my losses and added
a bus ticket to Vancouver
I promised him I would stop gambling
but I never did
                        and why would I
when it's always my falls that summon miracles
draw up enough compassion and grace
to bring forth angels

Piece of the action
the action's peace
drills a hole in the cranium
fresh air enters
      and all the pebbles are freed
          round and smooth
    from years
of circling
   in the skull

A good gambler knows the deck is unaffected
by conscience   history

he has no hunches
takes no insurance
doubles down
                         splits   aces
             not   faces
a good gambler can sit anywhere
won't blame the dealer or table position for his luck
takes a break from a losing battle
eats drinks   returns cold sober
          dopamine flow arrested

the good gambler just returns to his place
has no elaborate strategy
simply plays the odds

a million failed systems
warm his seat

Saturday night in the kitchen
I stood next to my father
as he played cards with my uncles
glasses of wine and old faded Italian cards
my father forgot me and I forgot myself
watching him play with his brothers
in the reconstructed piazza

each man enveloped in rules I didn't understand
perhaps a child shouldn't have witnessed
such thick smoke or shiny coins
they played to the following night
and because the game belonged to them
no one won or lost much
they snapped back to themselves
and smoothly returned to family and work

a different breed of men they were
than the ones I play with now
they go a full day without a washroom break
some players wear diapers
would rather shit in their pants
than miss a hand

I sometimes play in the basement
of an east end Chinese restaurant
we knock each other in the ribs at the cramped tables
a multicultural multiracial multilingual bunch
half the time we play poker
the other half we insult each other
in the other's tongue

to lose at poker is just self ignorance
opaque to yourself
            transparent to another
      one maximizes the bet
goes all in
shows 3 kings
and is ready to rake in the pot
when the player with the impassive face
who knows you better than you know yourself
          slams
down
          3 aces

at the end of the game the big winner
pulls out 50 bucks
takes the skinny white junky waitress
                her face full of welts
out through the back door
and nails her behind
the garbage bins

A slurred light
the Toronto morning
quietly suffers another stroke

I have tried to gamble myself
out of the city's disabilities
its cold weather and cement

Gerrard/Carlton/College
on my way home from the game
I stare out the streetcar window
an old homeless man without a fare
                        is kicked out of the vehicle
                into the routine slush

failures in black coats
                winter salt on their shoes
last night's bets and raises wander the city
some turn corners some climb up to Riverdale Farm
go across to the Necropolis walk around the graves
some trek over to Allan Gardens
lie on a greenhouse bench
and expire in the humidity

I have tried to rid myself of this city's inflexion
the gridded way of being

city that suspends
                examines   anatomizes urges
            instincts

nostalgia is hope walking backwards
my best memories are on the streetcar
it passes Women's College Hospital
and my crotch swells
                        across the street was Maloney's tavern
                        pick-up joint par excellence

what a slutty period the 70s
what guiltless promiscuity
multiculturalism at its best
interracial fluid exchange
bodies trading their diverse salts

we gyrated
                and throbbed away
the cold climate
melting the bland Toronto
        prose
            into a sweaty erotic poetry

the only game in town
                was body

now the thrill is all night poker
stop and start
                    blood through hardened
                art
                            eries
f ace cards clogging up the   heart

The sky is trying to resolve something
with all its cloud making

vehicle stopped at
                    word image
                              intersection
I nod off for a second and dream
against the cold glass of the window

I fight the monster
it's trying to steal my child
its face a scattered deck of cards
hag vulture snake jack queen king
then with my bare hands I tear off
                              a wing
                    and the bleeding thing
emits a human whimper
hobbles skyward
toward a mother cumulous

up to be
     re shuffled   re dealt

This was not her climate
beautiful Jamaican girl
        stuck here
    phrasing and rephrasing her poems

her paintings hard to lift
heavy with paint and vision

I was a teacher she trusted
and she read whatever I recommended
hoped I knew a title
that would save her life

she was caught on video stealing rope at a hardware store
not far from this stop they found her
dangling from a park tree
           a knotted branch
the brilliant girl voided
by our North

and just a week before her death
she gave me a mess of poems
which I placed under a pile of books

           I had my own issues
           debt divorce and child support
           was up most nights gambling online
           too tired too behind on my marking
           to edit a departure

           word
           a return

NOTEBOOK THREE

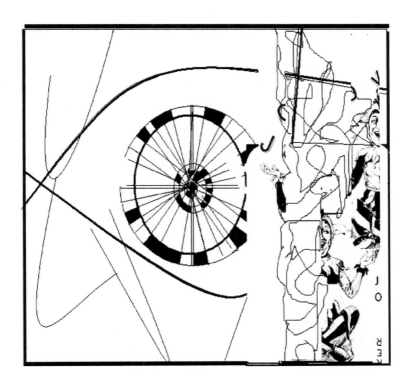

Big win means
an exit out of the solar system

reversal
of the flesh

                    jackpot is
                              the body's

                    sidestep
                         from itself

restart creation

ten dollars on the midnight
and the midnight came
                    paid 36 to 1
then I placed all my winnings on the line
and rolled the roll of my life
shot for 45 minutes
retrieving thousands of lost dollars
and more

the money didn't matter
what counted was how nothing becomes something
how a fish and loaf
multiply into
feast

The fire is seldom quelled
compulsion
is a wheel rolling away
                    from a burning wreck
you can't count on a cool hand touching
a fevered forehead

most gamblers would like to die at the table
win back anaesthesia
                    pre-natal coma

adrenalined forward
            through
            undeciphered
                    outer space
      escape from Copernican constraint
                heliocentric convention
                            enslavement to centre

Compulsion is passed on like a germ
transferred by storytelling the big win narrative
the guy who won the million dollar pot
more room more time
more space
    more pure
        blue sky

life speeded up
boring parts extracted
continuous tumble and roll
hope joy frustration grief
the experimenting heart testing emotional possibilities
in the artificial casino afternoon

toss the dice all the way to
fire memory the first big win
disappearance into the fever feel of it
coming seven come eleven the big bang
win it feel it coming the big feel coming the big is
just a matter of time space just a martyr to the big bang
feel it in the skeletal structure a subway train displacing
the marrow rolling yes across the no to all the yes its many
variations constant reinvention of the heavens new
sky friendly familiar the remote spaces folded in
wallet the imagination rolled back to original
size unclogged birth hole generating lush
season one springtime flaming across
the wager
gambler at the stake
burning up the
    world thrown
        into fever
the what-goes-up-must-come-down law
incinerated the
    body accountable to
   fiery serpent uncoiling
       reversing
          the brained eye
back to the first unmediated joy

Gamble speech

the lexical life savings staked
      hazard words
on what obliterates chance

toss the voice down
deeper than it should go
into the dead
and buried

blow out of this numbness
the morning toast is cold
        and the wet squirrel shivers on the top branch
for the old words have kept us
from catapulting
   over dull
      di vision
speak with dice in mouth
and be reborn
     double or nothing

tao ngue
spoken
  in action
  accelerate the
        nervous system back to
          language source

     les ondes
or
      osso
        blanco
          retirada del mar
            esperanto
e spiritu santo
the ancient romance
      delirio originale
         the bones retirada dal ciel

un coup de des
to end all chance
dice of the mouth

           undoing the madness of
   matter

perfectly sound
undoing

Accelerated voice speeding into vanish
vow to be carried
                over the
                        Falls
play a whole row of slots at Fallsview
run back and forth
between machines

see Niagara's liquid thunder crash down
        pounding resolve against
    the rocks

one compulsion ends
another one intensifies
inherent genetic predisposition
or blood flow
            electrical activity
or chemical wave
washing the brain

success is around the corner the gambler thinks
frantically moving from table to table   slot to slot
to pinpoint location of
                    swoon   amnesia   trance
the numbing affect

some take more risks after losing than winning
in an attempt to outrun the weight
return to original lightness

even the bystander is pulled in by the
gambling stories   false whirlwind enchanting the innocent
ringing whistling beeping hubbub blinking dizzying matrices
of colour   tossing dice perhaps for the last time
a sick old yellow man wears an oxygen mask
and who is to blame him
if just above and behind the eyes
                    is a listless prefrontal cortex
too lazy to tame impulses

Sanctuary of chance and danger
                              paddle wheel riverboat
fattened to be killed the gambler turns to luck for love and acceptance
immigrants mad for excitement
plantation owners
          cowboys
                         prospectors
the temptation to compound gain
the casino permits wins to set up losses
          early success increases eagerness to gamble

spilled coins   crowds   bells and whistles
food and drink   lights   music
carelessness   guessing
emotional kick   a croupier's call
the jingle of money the wild winning of others
rapid payout   mood arousals   jackpot size
illusions of skill   emotional involvement
gambles per minute   the longer the game the larger the bets

the trap is thinking that winning or losing are the same thrill
the trick is psycho management
to not regard money given by the house
as experimental platform
as windfall free to be risked

flirtation with jeopardy
the almost win propels the player forward
adventure beyond the customary bet
loss has its wild behaviour
                         the toss and its
unfathomable number of undeterminable variables
velocity trajectory
               air currents   gyro affects
                              angular momentum
          all make failure seem
                         accidental

Action gambler: controlling egotistical intelligent
attracted to skill games poker 21 horse racing backgammon
competitive from youth always with a system
and a personal ambition to outsmart
                              the rare bird Luck
                    pluck all its feathers
          he could never take a break
                    to reset the mind
                         cool the forehead
               look through the smoke
                              solve the fire

degree of compulsion
likened to degree of burn
was always tempted to double the bet
chase the loss
          blame it all on
               demon electro-chemical activity
                    brain is always betting
happens to everyone the risk
that topples everything
we're all wired for a loss of face
stole the petty cash and was caught
                    and as consequence lost everything the wife
                         the house the books the art

again night   again go   night after night   go again
21   21   21   sorry blackjack
dealer hot   all the time hot
21   21   21   sorry blackjack again
uncanny
          invariable fuck you
I'll try again
          try again   night after night
draw and bust   draw and bust
can't figure it   invariable   the dealer's advantage
but sorry sorry apologizes the dealer
                    uncanny how he
just pulls the right card   invariable night

after night
        go again
                go figure
go figure out   wrestle to the ground
pin down
            that fucking dealer's advantage

Escape gambler:

came with friends but now plays alone
started late in life   lured by luck games   slots   bingo
lottery   video poker   has her favourite machine
gets mad at it but can't resist the numbness
mother of children who no longer need her
cared too much   now dabbles
in self neglect

N O one ever wins Zeno argued that if space actually existed
it cannot be crossed could not be crossed the distance between
A and B between you and me your dust and your destination
can be infinitely divided half the distance half of half the way
then half of half of half the distance you would have to cross
through an infinity of halfway points to get to your dust endless
span of half way points supported by other endless half spans you
never arrive at what you want is on the other side of infinitely
divided dividing space you never reach or pocket the payoff
because winning is a house you can't visit it's a halfway house
ad infinitum that's why you can never touch your winnings must
reach through an infinity of half way points to collect the chips
can never touch them must cross an endless bridge of intermezzi
divided into interludes mediated infinitely multi-sectioned ever
sectioning desire never pocketed always let it ride ever and ever

Notebook Four

Game board diagrams etched into the slabs of temple roofs
carved into church pews
                concealed
in the grid underlying
the Necropolis

everyone plays prays to beat natural condition
even the deceased toss dice
attempting to outplay
                cause and effect
roll one afterlife after another

whether soul exists or not
the universe is dressed
in the fashion of its loss

boundless space
at its centre is a widow sun
a funeral procession of blind dumb spheres

and everywhere there are attempts to end the mourning
on cratered planets and moons
            in the games rooms   in the alleyways
      in schoolyards
dice are thrown against
the grieving cosmology

Word yanked me out of nothingness
            gave me a form unstable as itself

sentenced
            to entire body
I crave the weightlessness I was when I was only eyes
innocence that might return
a preliterate time when sight was trusted
where one knew what to love
just by looking
at its face

                the via negativa back to non-existence
                            splash in zero puddles

the exhausting energy
 presence
            requires

spades diamonds hearts clubs
are the 4 corners of a body's cancellation

tentative form in tentative space
perched on losses
                warbling
                            a clear toned
                disappearance

Came up to try my luck at this space time game to breathe in the
world's stench let me wait and see what happens perhaps this morning
will flow and the body will stretch out into one smooth federation of limbs
I talked myself into this unstable form brought up from nothing
into sun up sum down the need to fill empty husks tumbling
across the expanse and I'm tired sick of all this chance

I sometimes think it's easier to invite the terrifying hand
that I once fought off as a child
it came up under the bed
grabbed my ankle
            tried to yank me down
 into the floor

I wouldn't resist it now
that
elsewhere

        grip

A safe gambler bankrolls the game with intelligence
disciplines his face muscles
masters his eyes and the eyes of others
plays tight
        folds early

but a real gambler
lives for the short term
sidesteps the dispassion
goes for the speed
the heart pounding blindness
        plays to the last cent
never analyzes
his losses

                likelihood of royal flush is 2 598 960
                the likelihood of any hand is 2 598 960
                but it's the miracle randomly plucked from all the others
                that initiates the dizziness

delir   ious   gambl
                er
                        wild card   stalked by wil d cards
scat tered lines   swirls
no compass to cir cum
navigate the
                numbers   the numbness

get out of head
climb out
            spin

to
 what
is played for
        dreams come up
wild
assortment of urges

and joker
        jumped out at me
long and thin
loyal to the thinning process

too much body is practically
                    unholy
I must be whittled away
in the games room

nothing left
but nerve
        endings

A track and field of stolen drugs
his body a relay race of visions and highs
I heard his answer
to my question
                    what is the moon, Mike
he said *a hole in the sky*
and fell
        into his answer

Mike Urbansky rapture athlete
winner of the race
                ahead of me the length of one full absence
swimmer of the narcotic water
guest of waves and under currents
it took him many relapses
to fully drown

my every toss of dice is faint imitation
of his liquid
        self erasure

ROSS Walker was a bad gambler
never folded a hand
dangled his cards over the table
would accidentally drop them
    face up
          spoiling his
    bluff

termination of self by means of repetition
over and over again doubling the bet
yielding twice as much
          to
           departure
years of loss sent him constantly back to childhood
into the mattress
        the anaesthetic
storehouse

death/debt sent him letters
then rang the doorbell
then dissolved his lines
without calculating the odds
he saw every bet and raise
walked out without a cent of self preservation
            his soul spinning around the night
a tiny white ball
in search of double zero

his walls had an accusing stare
objects had eyes shadow people in all the corners
did not know why they were there
he studied what the philosophers poets saints said
about the angel with the
flaming sword
broken teeth black circles
of a slurring self
          sabotage
he spent days reading
he spent his nights shooting the dice
      hoping he could roll himself out

of space watching
went all in
dollar and syllable creature
he shook the bones and tried to make one monster
out of many eyes
and voices
a good gambler
takes advantage of the double down
                                    does not split
                        faces
but Ross Walker divided himself
plotting against his own exoskeleton
        trying to
air his guts

came to the last game flaunting a disaster pattern
the artistry of it when we found him dead
on a toilet seat at Ranch Billiards
pants and briefs down to his ankles
around his feet a meticulous composition
of dice   cards
            syringes

 and puke

A brazen broad daylight shooting in Little Italy on the crowd-
ed patio of the Sicilian Sidewalk Café during a Euro soccer match.
"The gunman looked clownish," a witness said, "he wore a hard
hat on top of a blond wig, a safety vest and a white filter mask."
Targeted and killed was a former member of a motorcycle gang
linked to gambling.

some do not fear water
some go under the waves and swim straight into the hit man's eyes

intense living dying
to bet on the oblivious not the obvious
to merge with the game be one of the verbs
                    a wheel's turn
                    a card's flip
                    a die's tumble

a gambler's death
            is debt collection
                    style of payment
bright beautiful sun and the families enjoying their meals
can't ward off
                    the sinkhole
        how the earth
opens up unannounced

BANG   BANG   BANG
and bullets penetrate a day crayoned in a kindergarten class
yellow sun and
too blue sky
                    three holes in the gambler's head
a shrieking widow   a friend or brother
crying
    John John oh John

the killer
   jumps
     over
       the metal railing
runs north on Montrose
     dust mask helmet
      goofy blond wig
disappears up the street
and into an alley

the corpse slumped against the brick wall
beyond luck and fortune now
still point and nucleus of all this panic and grief

BANG BANG BANG
the shots play back in my head
       brain
         bits
   hit the ground
gushing blood
the open and fluid skull
the dead man's thoughts pour
into street
     stain red octopus
        disentangling
from its own tentacles

but the blood spreads and the picture is unstable
the tragedy reshuffled
new shapes dealt
    strange suits
      face cards from
an unfamiliar deck

Johnny Maserati high roller
his wins losses
      ups downs
            kindnesses and cruelties
lie spectacular on the ground

the very red of dangerous living
blood mixed with strawberry syrup
my eyes licking the sweetness
of a life extremely lived

an existence in contrast to my own
for I gamble without risk of flesh or blood
my forfeiture barely visible
I risk only small amounts of vitality
surrender the will incrementally
extinguish discreetly

NOTEBOOK FIVE

The animal sees too much
                         eyes on each side of the head
two simultaneous pictures 320° of the horizon
is ever surprised by unexpected
                              events
libraries of air
when horses first meet they blow into
each other's nostrils

the signalling bulk
          tail position   swinging   clamped
lashing against the side
body of language   language of body
muscle tension

arched neck
impatient nodding   bared teeth
          ears pressed flat back
                         beware of kick

respect the beast for it like you requires other

even the shyest horse
when sick or dying will move dull-eyed
towards warmth

Meet the wind
on the ridge of a wave
glide play
        of liquid muscle

hypersensitive creature
responds to steady voice
      repeated words
          whistling cues

show it the boundaries
but if upset by sudden noise or movement
it will throw off uncertain
         rider

the animal is only partially understood
only the crude sounds are audible
   snickers
      neighs
        and snorts
the finer sounds are
archived in the animal's
        stature

And when a mounted cop rode through our street
it enlarged the day
            permission to stroke the animal's sides
                  to touch the mane of
                        magnitude
its long face and neck

I wanted to be the beast tall shiny energy
animal our origin
            childhood and love of speed
            the animal's stamina

when the apparition turned the corner   I galloped
                        up and down the sidewalk
                  clucking tongue
                  slapping thighs
vehicle of muscle and air
carrying invisible knights
and cowboys

If the animal should get jumbled
it rears up throws off
                      the rider
if the jockey is injured on the ground
it may kick him in the head
the hurt rider will be carried off on a stretcher

but if a horse is injured and thrashing on the ground
                 it is injected
              not euthanized
fully awake and paralyzed
suffocating and fully aware

a pretend death to make the crowd believe
the animal's at peace
carried out by a backhoe
then killed off track

Exactor triactor perfecta exacta
pay cheque on the line
the overloaded air doubled over by beer smell
                racing forms
        carpet the floor

at the wicket men purchase heartbeats
                        adventurous height
lean over a dizzy ledge
of racing muscle
speed
        sweat
lost dollars added up
            sins bundled and counted up
        a round figure
an oval track

a slow circle back to self
before one tears up
the losing tickets

In the excitement all is bent
bet on a horse that's not been sidetracked
that recently run and won
            win begets win loss is habitual
there's no room for adrenalin rush in the winning mind frame
only calm knowledge
                in the face
                        of muddy conditions

most bettors put themselves at the mercy
of fluctuating odds
false prices
            numbers that swerve and twist

bet on the firm number the
number that doesn't hesitate
the one known to spring to an early lead
takes the mud
                head on

only if before the start of the race
a horse's odds drop dramatically
bet on it
                those who know
                know something you don't

bet on experienced jockeys they understand the track
they know its signs tricks moods they can gauge the pace of a race
and remember the champion is always between
the long shot and the favourite

most people overlook the middle
in love with
                extremes
they make a complicated bet
when a simple one is best

one must have a clean head a clean nature
pocket the winnings and never
replay them

Thundering around the last turn into the stretch
ALL MY HOPE
running into
poor visibility
riding into a deep patch of fog
bears to the outside
 falters and fades
overtaken by PRESENT ENTANGLEMENT
and SHARP HUMOUR

close behind along the rail
        battling head to head
      UNACCOUNTED FOR and ALL I KNOW
just barely outrunning
  the onslaught

now coming from the outside
breaking from the pack
moving like a tremendous machine
        it's the unexpected result
99 to 1 SOMETHING OUT OF THE BLUE
crossing the wire
   winning by a nose

TWISTED HEART finishing last apparently limping
awkward from the starting gate
stale horse raced too young and hard
degenerated cells
                waste-laden blood
          hobbling home

Two colours very bright magenta pink
    or grayish green
injection in the neck

    good death
in a quiet open
                grassy area

control the fall reduce the reflex movements
will drop suddenly and go over backwards
mouth open and eyes rolled back
            loud exhalations and gasps
                    muscle tremors   jerkings
just death playing the reflexes
tinkering with its new toy
but no panic no pain
no trauma

if the veins can't be accessed
if the animal is thrashing
then death is through the skull

stand on slightly higher ground
point down towards the jaw
give a foot or two   breathe deeply
and squeeze the trigger

the horse is dead if the eye is touched
and there's no blink

a cremated horse yields 45 pounds of ash

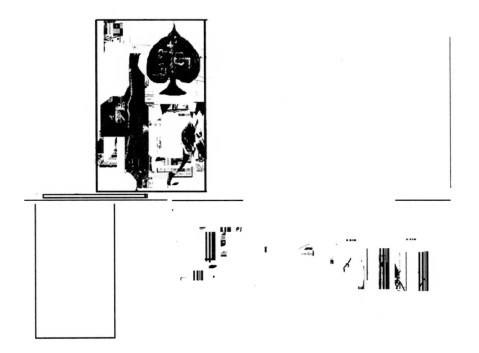

To intensify the competition
we each staked a valuable possession
Bill brought a painting
I an old book

the agreement was to play one game
no clock   the winner
                    leave with his prize

and the match was epic
equally skilled we proceeded
      with a
                        still intensity
considering
        reconsidering
strategies

lost in
moves ahead
                        without temporal junctures
                        aware only afterwards
that it sometimes took an hour
to move
a
   pawn

chess was our retreat   a monastic cell
a self absorbed meditation meditating only on itself
and it was the body not the mind
that abandoned the focus

by late morning Time returned
and barely awake
tired of the game
we reached a
stalemate

it was our last chess game
it was the last time Time left us
                        unsupervised

the night passed away
                faster than a finger's
        snap
then came the morning light
and like a love or passion that's come to an end
we folded the board
turned wine into water
and tossed
        the once so precious kings and queens
                        just mere plastic
into a torn cardboard box
returned to our lives
without winning or surrendering a prize

Everything spins
stellar solar lunar earthly rotations

everything satellite to a debt

punctual payments
to the dice and wheel

then return faithfully to a
spare apartment

indebted man
does not luxuriate
in comforts or convictions

expects no change

a future without unforeseen events

Doubling the bet chasing the loss
body converted to money
matter
        immaterialized

saint of compulsion penniless
sitting on top a minus column
I tidy up the living room
spend an hour cleaning   re cleaning
the circular glass coffee table

then I lie on the couch
flesh and mind stupefied
tucked somewhere between
TV   and sleep
I stay there all weekend

debt is not as simple as I thought
not a firm straightforward number
it presses against the optic nerve
a blind spot at centre vision

is a telescope
that does more than observe the heavens
but invents the remote dead spheres
it sees

is a sea weighed down
by its own salt

is a passing away calculating itself

3 AM is a marble head with blank eyes
the TV and the mind are without channels
a mental probe sent long ago to study the sky
returns with no report of life above

my little boy sleeps soundly in the bedroom
oblivious to the rotting beam
the sizable water stain on the ceiling

I pick off petals from the sick geranium
open the window and feed them to the cold air

        will the darkness in return
        spare me a nightingale
        will the creature fly to my potted plant
                cure it
        a full scale innocence
        singing what
        a beautiful bird
        am I

the icy pavements are seeded with slips and falls
and the pigeons minus themselves in the night air
vanishing one instinct at a time

the lighted office buildings above the houses
                square rectangular boxes
are evidence of my city's
failed imagination
a place that does not remember or forget

it doesn't matter
if I jumped into
            God
              or empty space
or if I
      died at the casino
I keep looking for an angle of escape
how to gamble myself out of this rock
immigrate to music
become a citizen
of the missing chord

The new day's clamor
noise of drill   engines   hammers
bottles dumped into recycling truck
transparencies crashing into other transparencies
transparencies crushed

a portion of the night's silence lingers on in objects
the cup on the nightstand
the statuette on the bookshelf
are one way mirrors
                       dead sciences
               observe me

the losing lottery tickets on the dresser are paper skies
tiny evacuated heavens with all the stars vacuumed out
what did I lose how much did I borrow
the dripping faucet is an indecipherable response
breakfast is the flavourless hole between earth and heaven
taste has disappeared the way a fist does
when the hands open

I look out the window to my neighbour's oak
the tree is impassive
I would like to be so reduced
but this universe did not include me in the vegetable kingdom
nor did it make me a dumb element
                   fluid
              mineral
                       gas stone dust
did not give me entrance into
the blank community

last night I dreamed *sharp stones broken shells*
led me to a hidden picnic
                   a family dressed in white
            sat between the cornstalks
invited me to share their food and comfort
a baby crow hopped happily
between the fallen crumbs

And then a second dream

beached on my lawn where at night I cool my feet
(the small patch of grass miraculously stretched into a playing field)
was a decomposing whale
                    a stranded sublimity
an exiled size
a deleted portion of the sea's magnitude
a proportion decommissioned by the universe

an evacuation of all the blessings ever bestowed on the animal
exited the blowhole
            a swarm of fireflies

had I known the water would creep this far inland
I would have moved to higher ground
avoided the putrefaction the meat and blubber decaying into
cracked icons and baptismal font
    broken pews
        organ pipes

and one of the eyes was an altar strewn with
                ashes and playing chips
                    scattered decks with disintegrating suits
evidence of a game terminated long ago
a smell of loss in the air
weighing down the atmosphere
    a failed and final gamble

My city is a diorama of debt
one moves forward with head down
reading the icy sidewalk as if it were
a ledger of owed sums

no child plays in this cold
draws patterns in the snow
reformats the winter

I live in a city where the mad are self sufficient
for decades now Fat Maria has slept
homeless in doorways
                    and yet she manages
to stay fat and alive
scabby elephant legs short skirts
no underwear big ass exposed to the elements
blotchy red face stuffed with food from garbage cans
she spits at nothingness
tells it to mind its own business

every day morning noon and night the same spot
in front of the Annex pool hall
Big Victor cigarette in hand and foot on car fender
talks Hungarian to an endless ear of air

a big income tax refund staked on one hockey game
in my misdirection of energy my spinning of bets
how am I any less insane than Victor or Maria
walking my daily circles the street is all I can afford

I noticed a new crazy person in the Annex today
a drunk indigenous man who argued with a large puddle
evaporate you fuckers
go back to your cloud
climb back home you motherfuckers
you gallons and gallons

Julian *can you show me east west north and south*
he looks hard at my face for clues
but finds no cardinal points

for months now I've been pointing out landmarks
from his mother's house the CN Tower is South
the park is North the school is East
the subway station is West
but at my house it all changes

nothing registers
he has no need of location
enjoys how things just magically appear
faithful and miraculous

       school
            park
                 home
             cat

it seems my hand is his only compass
a hand that holds cards tosses dice
throws away money and direction

my mind walks North
the feet walk South
I have just enough father in me
to keep eyes on the ground
and lead him around the dead bets
                the discarded decks
littering the way

Whenever we pass the man who talks to himself
at the corner of Markham and Bloor
I am not allowed to stop to listen to him

I'm sucked in by the intonation
the quasi Shakespearean magnitude of the fractured pronouncements
emphasis   compulsive repetitions
            random stress of
                    thoughts or phrases
I gather nothing
just fragments of a rage
against the world
and self

and why am I so intent on hearing this man
shouldn't I be afraid thinks my son
who wants to keep on moving urges me to cross the road
pulls me away from the soliloquy
concerned the language might
transfix me

he is just a child and immobility frightens him
sees how a human can become
a barking dog
                    expelled from the house
                            restrained to the yard
        leashed

to a voice

I look for coins in shirt or jacket pockets
under couch bed and bookcase
                    behind the radiator
and find enough money
to buy my little boy
a pizza slice and a treat

child in a narrow space between two houses
compressed between bricks
I pulled him out and gave him
a little metal train and he guards it jealously
all day long the toy is in his grasp

only when he sleeps is the grip released
and his small world falls from his hand

NOTEBOOK SEVEN

The casino is not built upon chance
its advantage lies in the certain long term game
comprised of countless asymmetries
10 000 tosses of the dice
a string of unstable elements
consolidating into a stable
profit for the house

unpredictable payoffs
meticulously designed
variable ratio reinforcement schedule
feeds the
        impulse-control disorder

magical intervention
wish making
lucky number
        rabbit's foot   cross
the seat you select
the dice you pick
where you cut the cards
illusion
                of choice

the more dapper gambler
thinks he can groom chance

near-miss misleads one into thinking
one is mastering the game

the bandit's one arm
        is unconnected to the
    internal machinery

No messages or appointments
no bushes to prune no snow to clear
just dizzy possibilities
multiplicity of bets
                eternal moment reshuffled   re tossed   re spun

I return by force of habit to bright light
overhead cameras see everything
the invisible is not welcome in casinos
not places for prayer
and yet the odd player will kiss
the crucifix dangling from his neck
whisper a request to the dice

Montecarlo   Biarritz   Baden-Baden
painted ceilings and chandeliers
I feast my eyes surrender my cash
and then a long flight home

the most honest casinos are in Vegas
the city wears the desert on its sleeve
Canadian casinos are the least hospitable
no free drinks and very stingy with their comps
when they sweep up a winning wager
or forget to pay the line
they ignore the complaint

casino dealers
        often gamblers themselves
knee deep in the blood loss
how do they justify their part
in the hemorrhage

Attended GA for a while
even thought I was cured
but returned to the dirty water

even Nature is compulsively disordered
the sky can't stop
making its clouds

impossible to uproot
the drive
to be
    reborn double or nothing
in
  chance

            return to the table
                win back the laminate flow
                    retrieve the soul
                        from unimaginable distance

to leave the casino is impossible
designed like a maze
no straight lines
                must twist
                    and turn
around tables and
            machines
                        until
                        a
                    game
                    entraps you

On my way to the roulette table I slide
around
     levers   tables
               the carpet's dizzying design

a slot player
dead or asleep in his chair
coins pouring out of the machine
but no bucket to collect a lifetime
of spinning pictures

at the wheel
the little white soul hostage to the wheel
               spins
                   falls
             tests a space it has already tested
settles for a moment
on black or red number
then spins again

It is the gambling urge concocts train bus plane car
free transportation always available
to and from the casino
oxygen pumped in
free drinks
        a fake wakefulness
a real debt

I go to the same dealers
because they cheat me
I can't tell exactly how
but my love for myself and my own
belong to the house now

I come to empty my pockets
hoping it will endear me to God
            who I've been taught
loves only the naked
and the poor

or I come to practice my art
              to draw a semblance of
        one's last moments
the ups and downs of a lifetime
crosshatched with every spun wheel
flipped card or rolled die

so that when death arrives
its features will be known

The rhythmic termination of self
every day same time same place same amount wagered
the ordinary staked to win the exceptional
the mundane catapulted into the void
far from the deformities of hunchbacked space

to devalue loss
the hundred dollar chip
                has the same size and weight
        of a dollar chip

I tested out a new sure-fire betting scheme
and maxed out multiple credit cards
then on my way home scrounged
for coins under the car seat
to pay the highway toll

Fallsview Casino overlooks Niagara Falls
a mist from the thunderous fluid climbs the hill
enters the gaming room
settles on the slots and tables
                a gambler
            seeks death but encounters fear
                begs the waterfall's mercy
and a few feet from the drop
is pulled from his plunge
brought back to his hard narratives not permitted to dissolve
                plucked out of the flow

suicide process starts
in the Fallsview lobby dismantling the mental frame
the oxygenated air the artificial light
the ironic escalator up to the Grand Hall
                        no ascent
                        but continuous downpour
                wears out the rock
the Falls are inching away
so too the inner voice erodes
            the mind's floor

Night bus home
back to Toronto from Fallsview
renewed vow to change one's life

body is the notebook
from it I rip out a lined sheet
write notes on loss and penury
                a naked
                        stop and skip
                                investigation
a week's work eaten by the wheel
record of the poor performance
analysis of the system
                breakdown

the view from the Burlington bridge is debt envisioned
night's subtractive flow
poisonous steel mill across the water
                        coal fire and smoke

is it me   is it me
but I think water is a far wide compulsive disorder
and all the drowned are medicine to heal
the sick redundancy of waves

to write away this gambling habit
too is part of the habit
obsession to know obsession
striving for perspective
mind contorts   positions
                        repositions itself
but pen drops

and I give up fishing barehanded in the cold stream
put up the hammock and sleep outdoors

        suspended

        in the losing pattern

Other Recent Quattro Poetry Books

Best New Poets in Canada, 1st edition

This is Why We're Made in the Dark by Justin Lauzon

a toast to illness by Corrado Paina

Fox Haunts by Penn Kemp

Panoptic by Tom Gannon Hamilton

Spenser by Carl Hare

The Heart of All Music by Stanley Fefferman

Vice Versa by Renée von Paschen & Robert Paquin

Brace Yourselves by Rocco de Giacomo

Out of Place by Kate Rogers

Odysseus by Carl Hare

A tattered coat upon a stick by Christopher Levenson

Perfect Day by Leif E. Vaage

Barbaric Cultural Practice by Penn Kemp

Hyaena Season by Richard Osler

Poet, Painter, Mountain: After Cézanne by Susan McCaslin

The Resumption of Play by Gary Geddes

Love Learned by Barry Olshen

Hermit Thrush by Mark Frutkin

Running on the March Wind by Lenore Keeshig

Midnight by Ian Burgham

Georgia and Alfred by Keith Garebian

Stone Soup by Kate Marshall Flaherty

The Hundred Lives by Russell Thornton

Night Vision by Christopher Levenson

Pin Pricks by Phlip Arima

Under the Mulberry Tree edited by James Deahl

Come Cold River by Karen Connelly

Beyond Mudtown by Rob Rolfe

And the cat says... by Susan L. Helwig

Against the Flight of Spring by Allan Briesmaster

The Rules of the Game by Ludwig Zeller

Too Much Love by Gianna Patriarca

parterre by elías carlo

Night-Eater by Patricia Young

Fermata by Dennison Smith

Little Empires by Robert Colman

nunami by Barbara Landry

One False Move by Tim Conley

Where the Terror Lies by Chantel Lavoie

Something Small To Carry Home by Isa Milman

jumping in the asylum by Patrick Friesen

Without Blue by Chris D'Iorio

When the Earth by Lisa Young

And tell tulip the summer by Allan Graubard

Book of Disorders by Luciano Iacobelli